Get A Life
(The Dummies Guide To Life)

Author Bill Rosoman

First Published 2007

ISBN 978-0-473-12855-5

Table of Contents

The Author, Bill Rosoman 2007

Introduction

Hi, Gidaye and Kia Ora.

This book grow out of my brushes with life and my life long study of and fascination with human nature. I also had a bout of cancer in 2006.

I find it interesting how people react to big events like finding out you have cancer.

Personally I believe you have to take the good with the bad and get on with it.

So I decided to write my thoughts down on my laptop and see what comes up! LOL

The opinions expressed are mostly my own with help from quotations etc.

I acknowledge every bodies copyright etc. But consider stuff on the internet free of copyright. Personally I like copyleft or creative commons licences.

Spirituality/Religion

Separation of church and state is a pillar of democracy.
NZARH

Religion is the opium of the people
Karl Marx

Politics and Religion are Obsolete. Now Science and Spirituality.
Neru

I have no problem with a small dose of Spirituality as I have seen it action whether in animals or in my past life living in a predominately Maori Community on the East Coast of the North Island of New Zealand.

My most classic example of spirituality in action was at a public meeting at the Kokiri Centre in Tokomaru Bay (is now the Kura Kaupapa Maori and the original building burnt down) The meeting was about adopting the new Charter for the Hatearangi Primary School of Tokomaru Bay. After giving out copies and me speed reading it, I asked the Question, "why does the charter having nothing about Wairua (Spirituality) when that is such a large part of Maori culture". Leone Collins (who I guess is part Maori and is married to one) asked what Wairua meant to which I replied, "If you have to ask me that then we have a problem".

At that moment a Maori carving fell off the wall into the middle of the room and everybody was amazed.

The Kokiri Centre was a Government funded scheme in the 1980s to create work for the unemployment schemes. It did some good as many public building and facilities were improved and renovated.

Having faith and Believing in ones self and humanity is good and healthy. Meditation connecting with ones inner being or soul can have many positive effects for human beings.

I do have a major problem with religion and the way it used as a crutch and a way of finding answers from divine being called god or Allah etc. Give me a break why rely on something that does not exist and is usually controlled by male gate keepers taking a buck on the way through and playing big power games as well as screwing all the little boys and girls or controlling women in the name of religion.

You may need some help from friends, family, professionals but religion is not the answer, but in fact compounds the problem and takes away self reliance and self discipline in handling life's ups and downs.

Living a good moral life

One can live a nice clean and moral life and be non-religious. Churches do not have a strangle hold and morals and the good life.

I consider I live a clean and moral life and treat others as I would hope they would treat me.

I do not steal, though I did convert my neighbour's wife (sorry). I am honest and up front about my past and life.

I certainly do not believe in god as he does not exist and can not stand the religious nutters who the more religious they get the less tolerant they are of people like me.

I would also like to know how I can blaspheme something I do not believe in!

But hey if religion lights your fire go for it!

Too this end I have created Bill's Alternative Ten Commandments.

Bill's Alternative Ten Commandments

1 Thou Shalt <u>not</u> worship god
2 Thou Shalt be happy and have a laugh a day
3 Thou Shalt not steal
4 Thou Shalt live life to the fullest everyday
5 Thou Shalt think only positive thoughts
6 Thou Shalt love thy neighbour
7 Thou Shalt always have your glass half full
8 Thou Shalt manage the things you can and change the things you can change, and not worry too much about things you can not change
9 Thou Shalt Seek fulfillness within thyself
10 THOU SHALT GET A LIFE!!!!

This is the old version LOL

Ten Commandments

1. Thou shalt have no other gods before me.
2. Thou shalt not make unto thee any graven image.
3. Thou shalt not take the name of the Lord thy God in vain.
4. Remember the sabbath day, to keep it holy.
5. Honour thy father and thy mother.
6. Thou shalt not kill.
7. Thou shalt not commit adultery.
8. Thou shalt not steal.
9. Thou shalt not bear false witness against thy neighbour.
10. Thou shalt not covet.

Major Events

"Life is not a journey to the grave with the intention of arriving safely in a pretty, well preserved body, but rather to skid in broadside, chocolate in one hand, a glass of wine in the other- thoroughly used up, totally worn out and loudly proclaiming "WOO HOO! What a RIDE!!!"
brilliant but unknown author.

Major events can have a major effect on people, some people seem to handle it Ok and others collapse into a deep depression and spend time saying "why Me" etc.

I have included my recent cancer story. I went to the Doctor and was told the news after test etc.

I consider it just one of life's hiccups. I was caught early and the cancer had not spread but even if it had, it seems and awful waste of energy to be crying, worrying and depressed about it.

The funniest moment was when I went to see the Cancer Society to see what they had to offer for cancer suffers. The nurse that spoke to me pussyfooted around to the point of insanity. In the end I said to her that I had no trouble with my mortality and to stop beating around the bush and give it to me as it is.

I keep telling my dear mum who is 88 now and my dad at 94 that sooner later things wear out and fall off and you have to die of something.

I guess in the end you have to have faith in your self in family, friends and in particular the health professionals.

All the people at the hospital have been fantastic from the Surgeon down to the lady doing the meals. I could not have asked for better care and attention. There is a lot of bull spoken about the public hospitals and it is all the Governments fault. But that is just not true and even if you chucked billions more dollars at hospitals, they would not cope. There is world wide shortages of nurses and doctors and medicines are insanely expensive, coupled with more and more interventions available and people living longer and we are coping quite well!

My cancer journey has been going on for 15 months and I have now had my bowel reversal operation and things seem to be OK.

Bill's Colorectal Cancer Journey.

Bill Had a bout of Colorectal (Bowel) Cancer,

In 2005 I had a bout of the Trots (going to the toilet quite often). I eventual went to my Doctor who was great. He gave me a quick examination and checked my Prostrate etc. He then referred me to the hospital and a specialist.

This is when the fun started. I have until this episode avoided the hospital for over 20 years. I had excellent service and was poked and probed by experts.

I had examinations, blood samples taken, colonoscopy, xrays using a Barium Dye Tracer etc. etc.

I was then interviewed by an Oncologist. His verdict was that I had stage III Colorectal Cancer
So it was recommended I have surgery. I next visited the Surgeon. He did examinations and scans etc. and in November 2006 I had a month off

work to have my Cancer Operation.

Plan A was to use key hole surgery and make 3 incisions in my abdomen and do it like that. But when I woke from the Surgery, they had to do plan B. This was a full incision and an Ileostomy (bring the end of the small bowel through the abdomen and have a Stoma and Stoma Bag). The large bowel had leaked at the repair, the bowel is stapled back together. See the pictures and explanations of this page. I had section of bowel removed and surrounding Lymph nodes removed.

I spent a week in hospital and 3 weeks recuperating.

Then it was back to the Oncologist and recommendations that I have Chemotherapy.

Chemo was mostly as a precaution. I could do nothing and have a 60% chance of surviving and a 2% chance to get run over by a bus. If I had chemo I increased my chances to 75% survival.

I had weekly injections for 6 months. This was a pain and I felt like a pin cushion! Some of the nurses had some difficulty finding a vein, but such is life!

When the chemo was finished I had a Barium Xray to make sure the large bowel had repaired properly and there was no leakage.

In September I saw my Surgeon to set a date will be set for the reversal of my Ileostomy. But there was a waiting list. (Had the reversal in November 2006 as it was beginning to hernia).

The Stoma is a pain in the butt! I have had a few disasters. I had a blockage of the stoma and a bout of gastroenteritis which was 3/4 days of a nightmare. My bag was filling every few minutes and I had spillages and bags bursting (Yuk).

Still every day above ground is a good day and a lot of my friends have died, including two I knew of bowel cancer. Most males leave it to long before seeking treatment. Mine was caught quite early and tests etc. to date show it has gone.

Computed tomography (CT), originally known as computed axial tomography (CAT or CT scan) and body section roentgenography

Colonoscopy/Sigmoidoscopy
From
Wikipedia, the free encyclopaedia.

Colonoscopy is the minimally invasive endoscopic examination of the large colon and the distal part of the small bowel with a fibre optic camera on a flexible tube passed through the anus. It may provide a visual diagnosis (e.g. ulceration, polyps) and grants the opportunity for biopsy of suspected lesions. Virtual colonoscopy, which uses 3D imagery reconstructed from computed tomography (CAT) scans, is also possible, as a totally non-invasive medical test, although it is not standard and still under investigation. Furthermore, this imaging technique does not allow for therapeutic manoeuvres such as polyp removal or biopsy. If a growth or polyp is detected using CT colonography, a standard colonoscopy would still need to be performed. Colonoscopy is similar but not the same as sigmoidoscopy. The difference between colonoscopy and sigmoidoscopy is related to which parts of the colon each can examine. Sigmoidoscopy allows doctors to view only the final 60 cm of the colon, while colonoscopy allows a complete examination of the colon, which can measure well over six feet (two metres) in overall length.

Barium meal/enema
From Wikipedia, the free encyclopaedia

A barium meal, also known as a barium swallow or an upper gastrointestinal series is a procedure in which radiographs of the esophagus, stomach and duodenum are taken after barium sulfate is ingested by a patient. Barium meals are useful in the diagnosis of structural and motility abnormalities of the foregut. There are two varieties of barium meal, these being single and double contrast meals. A single contrast meal uses only barium, a radiopaque (or positive) contrast medium, to image the upper gastrointestinal tract while a double contrast meal uses barium as well as a radiolucent (or negative) contrast medium such as room air, nitrogen, or carbon dioxide. The double contrast meal has the advantage of demonstrating mucosal details and is much more useful as a diagnostic test allowing the detection of small mucosal lesions such as diverticula or polyps.

A barium enema is given in order to perform an x-ray examination of the large intestines. Pictures are taken after rectal instillation of barium sulfate (a radiopaque contrast medium).
Stoma (medicine)
From Wikipedia, the free encyclopaedia

In medicine, a stoma (Greek - plr. stomata) is an opening, usually an unnatural or surgically created opening which connects a portion of the body cavity to the outside environment. One well-known form of a stoma is a colostomy, which is a surgically-created opening in the large intestine that allows the removal of faeces out of the body, bypassing the rectum, to drain into a bag or other collection device. The historical practice of trepanation was also a type of stoma.

Ileostomy
From Wikipedia, the free encyclopaedia

An ileostomy is a stoma that has been constructed by bringing the end of the small intestine (the ileum) out onto the surface of the skin. Intestinal waste passes out of the ileostomy and is collected in an external bag stuck to the skin. Ileostomies are usually sited above the groin on the right hand side of the abdomen. Bill

Well I am back and almost back to normal.

I had my operation on the 25th January 2007. I went in at 2pm, though there was a half hour delay while a nurse and two doctors tried to find a vein in my arm. It was quite funny! Eventually into theatre at 2-30pm and came too in ward 12 at 4-45pm.

While it was great not to have my bag any more I was now on a roller coaster of pain, sleep deprivation and getting my plumbing to work. What with the nurse taking vital signs all the time and trying to got to the loo, you also wined up being sleep deprived, but hey it is all moving n the right direction.

I will not bore you with all the gory details suffice to say it is a pain waiting to see when and if you plumbing is going to work. It is a matter of plenty of fluids and some food and wait and see. Still by Sunday I was making all the right moves.

I had a temperature Saturday so was kept in an extra day, but come Sunday I was discharged to my Niece's place in the afternoon.

Since being home I have been eating small meals, drinking lots and slowly am getting control of my body and now most of the pain is gone. I have the District Nurse visiting to keep an eye on me and changing my dressing.

I have a total of three weeks off work. I have also taking the time to get my van painted and start planning my life! It is amazing that now I can go places and do things that I have not been able to do for 14 months.

I am also trying to get back in to good sleep habits as I have not had a full nights sleep and it will be great to be able to sleep without having to worry about going to the loo.

Well I better have some breakfast and start getting organised and some work done. My Niece's IBM laptop died so will start with that I guess.

Bill

Motivation/Inspiration

Motivation/Inspiration are essentials tools in making life a positive experience and for coping with those moments of doubt in our lives.

I believe in the power of positive thinking and would call myself a **pessimistic optimist!** In other words I believe in being optimistic and positive but it has to be tinged with a touch of reality. There is only one Tiger Woods and one Bill Gates and the chances of another person doing the same things is slim, but positive attitudes and a clear vision of what you would like to achieve are certainly better than being depressed or seeing the world through a glass that is half empty.

I have included so quotes which I believe are good. I have personally seen John Kehoe in action at a seminar in Auckland and he is good and right. That to have change you need to start with your own consciousness and get your mind and body in order first before we can effect or create external change around you.

I also like Allan Pease known internationally as "Mr. Body Language" . I have seen him in action he is good. Body Language is very interesting except most people do not get it. I love playing body language with little kids it is fun.

In the long run, we shape our lives and we shape ourselves.
The process never ends until we die, and the choices that
we make are ultimately our responsibility.
Eleanor Roosevelt

You gain strength, experience and confidence by every experience
where you really stop to look fear in the face.
You must do the thing you cannot do.
Eleanor Roosevelt

No one can make you feel inferior without your consent.
Eleanor Roosevelt

Read motivation books Napoleon Hill John Kehoe

"Most great people have attained their greatest success just one step
beyond their greatest failure."
Napoleon Hill

Effort only fully releases its reward after a person refuses to quit.
Napoleon Hill

Who said it could not be done? And tell me what great victories does he
have to his credit which qualifies him to judge what can and can't be
accomplished.
Napoleon Hill Author of the 1936 classic..
Think and Grow Rich

Desire is the starting point of all achievement, not a hope,
not a wish, but a keen pulsating desire which transcends everything.
Napoleon Hill

Experience is an asset of which no worker can be cheated,
no matter how selfish or greedy his immediate employer may be.
Napoleon Hill

Cherish your visions and your dreams as they are the children
of your soul; the blueprints of your ultimate achievements.
Napoleon Hill

Do not wait; the time will never be "just right." Start where you stand,
and work with whatever tools you may have at your command, and
better tools will be found as you go along.
Napoleon Hill

The strongest oak of the forest is not the one that is
protected from the storm and hidden from the sun.

It's the one that stands in the open where it is compelled to struggle for its existence against the winds and rains and the scorching sun.
Napoleon Hill

When defeat comes, accept it as a signal that your plans are not sound, rebuild those plans, and set sail once more toward your coveted goal.
Napoleon Hill

Mind Power, John Kehoe
What we imagine, concentrate on or visualize in our minds will actually manifest into reality.

About Mind Power
John Kehoe's Mind Power system is a practical course which helps us to achieve our goals.

Looking to Change Your Life?
If you want to make changes in your life, you must look to the cause, and the cause is the way you are using the conscious mind - the way you are thinking. You cannot think both negative and positive thoughts at the same time. One or the other must dominate. The mind is a creature of habit, so it becomes your responsibility to make sure that positive emotions and thoughts constitute the dominating influence in your mind.

In order to change external conditions, you must first change the internal. Most people try to change external conditions by working directly on those conditions. This always proves futile, or at best temporary, unless it is accompanied by a change of thoughts and beliefs.

Awakening to this truth, the way to a better, more successful life becomes crystal clear. Train your conscious mind to think thoughts of success, happiness, health, prosperity, and to weed out fear and worry. Keep your conscious mind busy with the expectation of the best, and make sure the thoughts you habitually think are based upon what you want to see happen in your life.

Water takes the shape of whatever container holds it, whether it be in a glass, a vase or a river bank. Likewise, your subconscious will create and manifest according to the images you habitually project upon it through your daily thinking. This is how your destiny is created. Your life is in your hands, to make of it what you choose from.

An Introduction to Mind Power

What Is It That Makes a Person a Winner?

"It's all in the mind," says Arnold Schwarzenegger. Newly appointed Governor of California and multimillionaire, successful real estate tycoon, movie star, body-builder and five-time winner of the Mr. Universe title, Arnold has it made. But it wasn't always so. Arnold can remember when he had nothing except a belief that his mind was the key to where he wanted to go.

"When I was very young, I visualized myself being and having what it was I wanted. Mentally I never had any doubts about it. The mind is really so incredible. Before I won my first Mr. Universe, I walked around the tournament like I owned it. The title was already mine. I had won it so many times in my mind that there was no doubt I would win it. Then, when I moved on to the movies, the same thing. I visualized myself being a successful actor and earning big money. I could feel and taste success. I just knew it would all happen."

The technique Arnold is talking about, the technique that brought him so much success, is called visualization. Visualization is using your imagination to see yourself in a situation that hasn't yet happened, picturing yourself having or doing the thing you want, or successfully achieving the results you desire.

Let's say you want to be more confident. Using visualization you picture yourself working, talking to people, all with great confidence. You imagine yourself in situations that normally give you difficulty and you see yourself in these situations as confident, at ease, and performing well. You might picture your friends and associates complimenting you on your newfound confidence. You feel the pride and satisfaction of being a confident person and in your mind you enjoy the things that happen to you as a result of your confidence. You visualize everything that would or could happen to you and live as if it really is happening to you.

Any thought put into your mind and nourished regularly will produce results in your life.
What is it that you want in your life? Better health? Then get health consciousness. Greater prosperity? Get prosperity consciousness. More spirituality? Get spirituality consciousness. Everything exists as a possibility. All that's required is for you to feed in the necessary energy until your objective becomes your own.

How reassuring it is to think that no matter what a person's past or present situation, no matter how many times he or she has previously failed, if that person would but regularly feed his or her consciousness, his or her situation would change! This remarkable ability has been given to each and every one of us to use or to ignore. It costs no money. It takes no special talent. It takes only the decision on your part to take the time and put forth the necessary effort to develop the appropriate consciousness. That's all! Everything else will automatically fall into place.

Motivational and Inspirational Quotes by "Napoleon Hill"

If you cannot do great things, do small things in a great way.

No man can succeed in a line of endeavour which he does not like.

Persistence is to the character of man as carbon is to steel.

What we do not see, what most of us never suspect of existing, is the silent but irresistible power which comes to the rescue of those who fight on in the face of discouragement.

The majority of men meet with failure because of their lack of persistence in creating new plans to take the place of those which fail.

The most interesting thing about a postage stamp is the persistence with which it sticks to its job.

Get a Life

This is the rub and were I am liable to go right off the scale!

I mean get a life, take control of your body, mind and life and if things are not going that great sit down and make a plan to turn things around and get a life.

You can not blame god, the Government, the weather, if you have had an illness or a traumatic event in your life, you need to dig into yourself and with the help of friends, family and professionals you can get through it and have a great life.

So I guess what I am saying life's a bitch or a beach and then you Die, but in the mean time you need to get a life. Get out there and grab life by the tail and give it a good shake and see what happens.

Now that my operations for my cancer are over, I certainly plan to get a life and use my campervan to get out and about. I have five weeks outstanding and from this year in New Zealand we get four weeks annual leave. So I plan to take a four week trip to Gisborne and the East Coast to visit friends and my old haunts though it is mostly sad memories now. I want to get some videos of the places I I used to live in and visit. Maybe in 2008 I would like to go to Australia and visit the Formula 1 Motor Races or an international Cricket or Rugby match. I have not been overseas since 1979 and have not flown on a Jumbo Jet yet.

So I am certainly going to take my own advice and get a life before it is too late LOL.

Some Do's and Dont's

> Remember the Glass is always half full
> Stress relief is music, diet and exercise
> A Maori saying, "Me huri whakamuri ka titiro. whakamua" In order to plan for the future, we must look to the past
> The past is in front of us. - Maori saying
> Deal with the past but do not dwell there
> Get a Life
> Make small steps forward each day
> Keep busy but take time out to contemplate/think
> Do different things
> Doing the same things will get the same result
> Seek friendships
> Join a club/activity
> Stop feeling sorry for your self
> A journey of 1000 kilometres begins with the first step
> Learn from history
> The Human mind is amazing
> Get a hobby/interest
> Do not think negatively

  "No" means not yes yet.
  Pamper yourself now and then
  Do not take life too serious have a laugh now and then.
  Persistence Overcomes Resistance
  If all else fails take a Lotto ticket?
  Life is a challenge and full of possibilities
 Talking to friends and family is good for the soul

All the wonders you seek are within yourself
Thomas Browne

I woke in 1986 and said "From today I am going to think positively, and the most positive thing I can do today is get a divorce" That is despite the fact I did not want to get a divorce, but my marriage was getting very rocky.

A friend used to get raped regularly by her father, she said that she transported her mind and spirit to a lovely field full of flowers and birds.

A little sincerity is a dangerous thing, and a great deal of it is absolutely fatal.
Oscar Wilde

AFFIRMATIONS

The possibilities of thought are infinite, its consequences eternal, and yet few take the pains to direct their thinking into channels that will do them good, but instead leave all to chance.

I am convinced that people that spend all day depressed and worry about their life, wind up with their brains hard wired for the worst of life. I am also convinced that the reverse is true. If you have nothing but positive thoughts and a positive outlook on life then good things will mostly happen.

And of cause western medicine only treats the symptoms and not the cause. You get given a label of Bi-Polar etc. and wind up on horrendous medication.

Spending time looking at all the bad things of life are for me a complete waste of energy, the same as I try and tell my Nieces and Nephews that is not such thing as **can't** As soon as you say I can't do something you have put up a brick wall and you will probably fail. How about saying I do not know how or the job is too big for me, but I can find out how to do the job or I will get someone to show me and help me.

Therefore for me there is no such word as can't!

Sure I make mistakes and break a few things, but hey if you never try new things or give things a go what sort life are you going to live?

Society is so *risk adverse* nowadays it is not funny. While kids will be kids and broken bones etc. will happen, to say kids can not play outdoors or give life a whirl are ridiculous and in the end counter-productive as we wind up with a society of wooses nandypamy people afraid to step out of their comfort zone ever and what a dull place that would be!

Stress Reduction

Instructions
1. Place Kit on a firm surface
2. Follow the Instructions in the circle above
3. Repeat step 2 till stress ceases or you are unconscious
4. If unconscious cease activity
5. Stress is relieved

Bill Rosoman guru@nzenterprise.com 2003

It is the same with travel, when in Rome do as the Romans do I say. Try new things and food and give life a go. Current generations strike me as McDonald's and Burger King junkies, and will not try new things or new foods. Some of my favourites foods are Maori Porridge i.e. Rotten Corn with cream and sugar. Fillet Mignon and Boysenberry Parfait are my favourite western foods. I refuse to eat McDonald's hamburgers as I do not consider them food.

Quadruple Bottom Line

I believe in the Quadruple Bottom Line.
It involves;
Cultural/Spiritual; Social; Environmental &; Economic wealth

I believe it applies in Companies and Corporations as well as Government Departments and ones Personal Life.

You need to look after your Cultural/Spiritual needs as well as your Social and your Environmental situation and Economic Wealth.

It is like a big puzzle without all the pieces you can not complete the puzzle of life!

If you are living in a violent situation for instance then you need to address that issue to complete the puzzle.

I believe that in the 21st Century we are going to have face some stark realities especially to do with the environment and global economics. The Americans are going to have to learn one way or another that they are not the worlds police and that not everyone wants the world the way the Americans do. The American way of life sucks and there version of capitalism certainly sucks. Instead of spending zillions on the war on terrorism and hating the world which in return hates America and some with a real vengeance they could spend ten percent of what they spend on war on loving the world then we may see a difference. I believe in Democracy and Capitalism but it is the version I quibble over. I like the English version of Democracy were the Head of State (currently the Queen, though I would prefer a President) has mostly ceremonial powers, though she can act sometimes as well. The Prime minister is just a member of parliament and does have limitations. Not like in America were the President has very large powers and some he can exercise without referral to Congress.

I also prefer a Socialist version of Capitalism were wealth is spread much more evenly and there is not the huge gap between the rich and poor. America is a glaring example of the gap between rich and poor. On the one hand you have Walmart employees on a pittance of $15,000 a year and taking a class action against Walmart for better wages, and there is 26 million Americans below the poverty line and can not afford medical insurance (though some states like California are trying address this) and on the other hand you have guys like Bill Gates plundering the world and then giving billions to his charity which I think is really really bizarre. I mean he could actually give Windows software away for free and would make his money from MS Office etc.

Personal I do not use Windows but Linux Kubuntu which is provided free by a South African Billionaire who lives in the USA. He still makes money from it as well by providing corporate services around Ubuntu/Kubuntu and gets the global community to contribute software, documentation and free development of the software he provides for free. I personally feedback by putting up a website and providing documentation about what I have done and what worked for me.

So Kubuntu Software is a way of providing a Socialist version of Capitalism to help people instead of just taking all the money you can and then setting up a Charitable Trust to give it away too. I mean why rip people off in the first place if like Linux Kubuntu you can actually give stuff away and still make money out of your endeavours.

The Americans also have to learn that you can not just consume and to hell with tomorrow, though I am encouraged by the new 2007 Congress being dominated by Democrats who are at last having the courage to ask questions and face the realities of life. I always said from day one that America would win the war in Iraq hands down but would never win the peace. If George Bush had taken just a little look at history he would have left Iraq alone. He would have seen that Iraq may be the cradle of civilisation but they have also wiped the arse of invaders like the British only 80 years or so ago and the Americans face the same issue. More arms and more money and being a Super Power do not guarantee success in places like Iraq or Vietnam.

The Americans never seem to learn! BTW This rave is not anti the American people but their Government and the way they are patriotic to the ridiculous and wind up getting a bloody nose cause they think that might is right.

America and a large part of the western world are going to have face reality and get a life.

The WTO rounds are going to get nowhere as long as the USA and the EU continue to pump billions of dollars/Euro into farm subsidies and expect the rest of the world to have no barriers to trade and services. I think the most evil WTO thing is TRIP, Trade Related Intellectual Property Rights. This treaty is manipulated by countries like the USA by extending copyright for 70 years (to help Disney out) were in New Zealand it is 20 years, and being able to patent ridiculous things at the drop of hat. Then to bleat when people break copyright and burn software and movies till their hearts content. It is nuts and defies logic if compared with the philosophy behind the example I have given with Linux OS Software. Having strict copyright and patents can actually be counter-productive and stifle the very entrepreneurship the western world craves for. The USA also censors the Internet just as China does to stop Americans viewing stuff like abortion and downloading stuff like music and this in the land of the supposed "FREE".

Get a Life I say!

For me these issues are also part of the puzzle of life but looking at

the big picture.

Laughter is the Best Medicine

Seriously, scientists have found that laughter is a form of internal massaging that exercises the body and stimulates the release of beneficial brain neurotransmitters and hormones. A positive outlook and laughter are actually good for your health! If you haven't read Norman Cousin's book on this, you should.

Adults laugh approximately 15 times per day, while children laugh about 400 times a day! When we grow up, somehow we loose a few hundred laughs a day. That's sad. And it can be life threatening.

Did you know that a good belly laugh gives you the same benefits as an aerobic workout? Laughter boosts the immune system and lessens pain, and it also reduces stress, lowers blood pressure, and has a beneficial effect on our overall well-being. Laughter may also help protect you against a heart attack; this has important implications in societies such as the U.S. where heart disease remains the number one killer.

We know that exercising, not smoking and eating foods low in saturated fat will reduce the risk of heart disease. Perhaps regular, hearty laughter should be added to the list. Ah, but that doesn't sound very mediciny, eh?

So, How many psychiatrists does it take to change a light bulb? Only one -- but it will take a long long time, and the light bulb has got to really want to change.

Thanks
http://www.drellenrudolph.com/psyessay2.html

Redundancy

I worked for 23 years for the New Zealand Post Office later to be Telecom. In the 70s and 80s they employed 30,000 people and as a Government Department it was very over staffed and inefficient. It then became and State Owned Enterprise (SOE). They did a master plan which basicly was to get rid of staff. We were offered voluntary redundancy! I wrote and asked how much would I get they wrote back and said you have been accepted. We were sent to a seminar about redundancy and how to cope with depression etc. They had a scale and over 100 points you were in suicide country. In 1988 the year of my redundancy, I got divorced, I lost my favourite cat and was made redundant, that was 150 points. So I said to our welfare officer who was taking the seminar, how come I am not dead and while I understand what you are saying, give me the money and let me out of here. I also met an ex-Telecom guy I knew pumping petrol and said "what was it like", he said. "like getting out of jail". So I took the money and was self-employed for 11 years. The sad thing was that the welfare officer shot himself even though he would have made more money on the unemployment benefit.

I decided to get a life and get on with it. My glass is always half full and you have to see everything as an opportunity,

While I always new I would not make as much money and in 1999 my business was closed down due to lack of money and taxes owed, I still consider I was successful for those 11 years. Currently I am employed as a cashier at a petrol station, which is good as it pays the bills.

Rights and responsibilities

People nowadays are very quick to assert their rights but not quite so keen on their responsibilities.

The younger generations seem to think they can do almost anything without fear or consequence when clearly as Einstein said every action has an equal and opposite reaction.

Farmers are the same they keep bleating how they have rights with their land, when plainly their land title says the land is held in "fee simple" meaning they have some rights and a lot of responsibilities toward the land and environment and people and animals as well, and can not do anything they wish and to hell with the consequences.

It is good to know your rights and stand up and be counted when it counts, but also it is good to know your responsibilities.

I have over the years been involved in tackling things like incest and paedophiles. Paedophiles seem to have a warped sense of reality and never admit their mistakes, never take any blame or any responsibility for their actions, and say things like "she asked for it" or "she consented", when clearly an under-age person is not capable of giving informed consent and that is why we have laws against this type of offence.

A few seconds of sexually gratification for the perpetrator leads to a lifetime of misery for the victim and their family.

You need to know your rights but also be aware of responsibilities and the consequences of your action, some of which may be unforeseen.

It is sad we have an open society, but still have people who think laws and norms of society do not apply to them.

It also confounds me when people commit crimes and must know that they will sooner or later be found out. But I guess if your thoughts are already warped then you give little regard to the consequences of your actions.

Sometimes you maybe down because of the way you are being treated by someone or say a Government Department. Then it is good to know your rights and can tackle the problem head on and solve it. The best way out of a problem is through it. It is also good to tackle the problem head on as to not address the issue tends to let it stew in your mind and eat away at you, tackling the issue especially if you have some sort of victory is good and empowering.

There can also be a lot of speculation on both sides of an argument if people and organisations do not sit down and work through problems and come up with a solution that hopefully is a win, win situation, or at least solves the problem so people can move on.

Many Government Departments are powerful and have many laws to invade your privacy and rights, but they also responsibilities and need to be mindful of the their powers and the consequences these have on the people they are dealing with.

Inland revenue are a classic and have caused people to commit suicide etc. But they can also be beaten.

I have tackled inland revenue twice and had victories despite their size and powers.

Once was when I ran computer training courses in the 19080s and inland revenue lost the link between our operation and our parent body a Trust in Gisborne. I am sure it happened when they installed new computers. Anyway the guy kept threatening me with a fine of $3000. I asked him to reply to eleven points I had made in a letter to them. They just kept threatening. So I went to what they had then a Public Advocate. I showed him all the documentation and he said what do you want. I said I want inland revenue to take to court so I can prove them wrong and make them look like idiots and I have the facts to back it up. I also want this guys head on platter and I will get it. I never heard another word about it.

In the 1990s my business was not doing too well and I got behind with my tax returns, but inland revenue were making mistakes as well. They started threatening me and say they would sell my car and boat etc.

I did sell my house and pay my bills. I went to inland revenue and was interviewed by a front line staff person, Alison. She showed me a list of assets I could sell etc. and pay my debt. I said it was not that easy and I needed to talk to a senior member of staff so we could sit down and sort it out. I also said that according to the inland revenue act of 19 whatever and section so and so. The Commissioner at his discretion can right off tax if it is going to cause severe hardship or is deemed unreasonable. I asked her to concentrate on these issues. She said it could not be done, but went and sort advice, some 20 minutes later she reappeared with her jaw to the floor saying you are right, but still would do nothing about it.

The next day I wrote an Allan Pease letter, were you state in big text what your issue is and what you want done about it.

I said "the lady that interviewed me yesterday was ignorant, arrogant and divorced from reality and I demand a review from a senior officer".

I hang on this for 18 months despite repeated threats and finally got a review and solved my problem in a month or so and when I filed my tax returns, all the tax was written off at the strike of a keystroke by the senior officer.

While I cried at the final interview with inland revenue it was through the relief of having them off my back and having solved my situation in basically a win win situation. There was no mileage in them coming after me for a few thousand dollars I did not have as it would cost them financially and publicity wise than it was worth. I was also finally able to get on with my life and concentrate on rebuilding my life in a new town with new opportunities.

You too can get a Life!!!!!!!!!

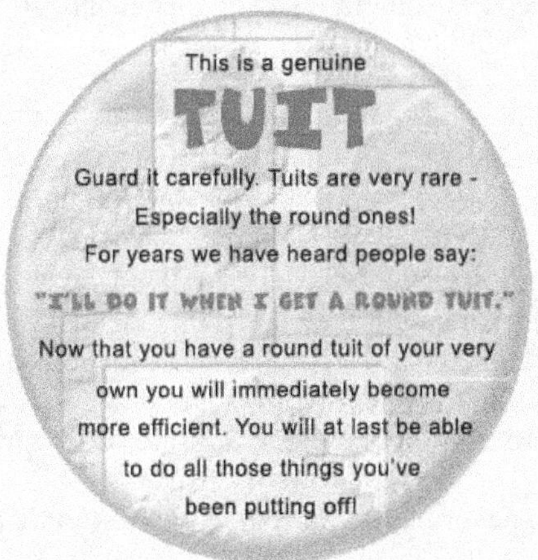

Placebo
From Wikipedia, the free encyclopaedia
(Redirected from Placebo (origins of technical term))
For other uses, see Placebo (disambiguation).

A placebo is a medicine or preparation which has no inherent pertinent pharmacologic activity but which is effective only by virtue of the factor of suggestion attendant upon its administration. The substance may be ingested, injected, inserted, inhaled or applied.[1]

(The article quoted from here distinguished medical placebos (described here) from the medieval meaning "unwelcome guest at funeral meal".)

The term placebo effect (as distinct from the more correct term placebo response) was introduced by T. C. Graves in 1920 "because it is the subject that has the subject-centred response. It is not the administered substance that generates the observed effect." (See below).

Sometimes known as non-specific effects or subject-expectancy effects, a so-called placebo effect occurs when a patient's symptoms are altered in some way (i.e., alleviated or exacerbated) by an otherwise inert treatment, due to the individual expecting or believing that it will work. Some people consider this to be a remarkable aspect of human physiology; others consider it to be an illusion arising from the way medical experiments are conducted.

A placebo is sometimes called a "sugar pill" in informal writings for the general public to quickly say that it has no useful medicinal content.

The human mind is extremely powerful and can do amazingly good things or bad depending on your thoughts and surroundings and the support received from family friends and professionals.

An example I have is when I lived on the East Coast and at the local hospital we had in the 1970-80s Doctor C and Doctor D. Both were well liked doctors partly I believe because they always gave out a bottle of pills. I think a lot of the pills were placebos i.e. sugar pills sometimes red sometimes green maybe. Everyone was happy.

People never plan to fail, they just fail to plan!

Plan something positive for your life some immediate goals that you know you can achieve. Maybe some exercise and giving up smoking. Maybe some financial goals, whatever you wish to achieve.

Self Reliance and Responsibility
In the end your life is determined a lot by your actions and you taking control of your own destiny. Luck or chance have very little to do with it. Luck is mostly what decisions you make and the actions you take to make your life great and exciting and feeling as though you are achieving your goals, aims and ambitions.

Acknowledgements

I acknowledge my friends, family and humanity.

I maintain in an innate belief in myself and humanity. I have since the age of eight, and was forced to go to church and saw the hypocrisy of the people and the institution of Christian religion, lived by a simple honest code of ethics and on the whole have not strayed from them.

I acknowledge every bodies copyright etc. But consider stuff on the internet free of copyright. Personally I like copyleft or creative commons licences.

BTW No Offence is intended with the comments made in this book.

Thanks http://www.lifepuzzle.com

To Lead a Happy Life

I Will never use the word "Can't" Again
Saying "can't" all the time is just a barrier and an excuse not to do or try things

I will not assume or imagine negative things happening
Most assumed or imagined things will never happen so why think them

I will learn new things and grow each day
Every day above ground is a good day and to learn new things is to progress forward

I will relax and take six deep breaths if I feel I am in a stressed situation
Instead of panicking or thinking bad things will happen, relax and take six deep breaths, the effects are good for mind and body

I will only think happy thoughts
If you say from today I am going to be positive and only have happy thoughts your life will change for the better

I learn some meditation techniques
Meditation is great and clears the mind of negative thoughts and negative energy

I will relax several times a day and have a power nap
Just find a quiet space and close your eyes, think of something nice and then relax your body, starting at your head.

I will get a life
If you approach life with a positive outlook you will be reward with a relatively trouble free life and a worry free life

Bill Rosoman
2007

About Bill Rosoman

Bill was born in Wanganui, New Zealand 23rd May, 1948.

His childhood was the usual working class suburban childhood, caring parents, three meals a day etc.

Bill was extremely shy in his youth partly maybe due to being beaten on his first day at school, for being left handed. Good old Mrs Ashton, Infant Mistress at Gonville Primary School kept at it every day till I was forced by brute force to become right handed. In the end it did Bill a favour, it made Bill ambidextrous, mentally tough and a true multitasker and a natural left and right brain thinker.

In 1970 Bill travelled to Western Europe and North Africa (Morocco), on his return he went to Tokomaru Bay 100km north of Gisborne on the East Coast of the North Island of New Zealand on promotion as a Foreman in the Outside Plant Division of the New Zealand Post Office (Telecom).

Europe certainly opened Bill's eyes to the other parts of the world and to other cultures, languages etc.

In Tokomaru Bay he was given the key to a Landrover 4 wheel drive vehicle and let loose, with no maps, no radio or cellphone and not a clue of were to go or how to fix a telephone (they were wind up Manual ones). 95% of the roads were not sealed and the telephone lines were usually a pair of wires strung up on telephone poles sometimes up to 50-60 kilometres long, with Party Lines of sometimes 4-6 houses on the one telephone line.

Tokomaru Bay made a man of Bill and he became a total extrovert! In Tokomaru Bay you were treated as an individual and it is when they stop talking about you, you started to worry!

Bill really loved the East Coast and spent from 1970 to 1999 in the region. Bill married a local (Ngaire Dewes, 1979 to 1988), was treasurer of the Rugby club, trustee of his Marae Te Ariuru (an honour for a European), Secretary of Tawhiti Blocks (5000 acres of undeveloped Maori land), member Waiapu Arts Council and on various committees etc.

In 1999, economic necessity drove Bill to sell the house he built in 1979 and to leave the area and eventually the region seeking employment.

From 2002 to 2007 Bill is working and living in a Campervan in the Hamilton/Waikato Region of New Zealand with trips to Gisborne and the East Coast to meet my many friends in the region.

October 2007

Email nugrownz@yahoo.com.au
Website http://www.webng.com/leftfieldnz/
Telephone +64-21-233-5427
Skype leftfieldnz

Ka Kite Ano for now!

NOTES

**Get A Life
(The Dummies Guide To Life)**

By Bill Rosoman

Life is Not a Dress Rehearsal

**You only get one shot
so you need to make the most of it!**

**You need to look within yourself
and see how you can make your
life a positive experience.**

**I hope this books helps a
few people having
a tough time with life.**